A Childhood Unshared

The Crumlin Poems

| *Illustrations:* | **Pauline Fayne** |
| *Copy editor:* | **Jennifer Fayne** |

ISBN 978-0-9519412-3-2

Acknowledgements and Thanks

We would like to thank our publishers,
Dominic Taylor, Revival Press and Mike Byrne,
Stonebridge Publications, who originally published some of the
poems in this book.

Special thanks are due to Jennifer Fayne for her computer and
editing skills, as well as her endless patience. Thank you
Thomas Fayne for solving the algorithm!

We are both indebted to our families and friends for their
patience and support.

Teri Murray and Pauline Fayne

September 2015

Table of Contents

Introduction

I met Teri Murray in Tallaght in 1988, where I was facilitating
The Clothesline Writers group. We quickly discovered we had a
lot in common; we both had young children, wrote poetry in
our kitchens or in any place and at any time we could. It was
some time later that we discovered we had both grown up in
Crumlin and shared many memories of local characters in the
area. In fact we had even both visited and played in the home
of one family in the area. We have shared similar childhood
experiences and written poems on similar themes, including
our Crumlin past.

After many years of friendship it seemed inevitable that we
would link these poems in a shared collection. We hope you
enjoy reading them.

Pauline Fayne

August 2015

The Poet Dreams of Crumlin

For Teri Murray

Childhood strangers, adult friends
we find the common ground
of our Crumlin past

Speak
of the turf depots earthy smell
the piling of damp sods
into shopping bags,
old prams
and the willing arms of
small children.

Laugh
at the convenience
of the off-license
attached to the post office -
quick step from pension queue
to counter
for a snipes of Guinness or
a baby brandy, small
comfort
against the creeping cold of daily life.

Remember
large families in small rooms and
how we longed to share
their 'Waltons' style lives -
blued white shirts
flapping on long lines,
overflow of clothes
flower bright on privet hedges,
steam of stockpots
and fresh baked bread
obscuring kitchen windows from our jealous gaze.

The shock of recognition
in each others words -
the dream lives and perfect homes
born between the pages
of the books that sustained us,
the same envied neighbours, the one
need to belong.

Now we return
turn down quiet streets
and empty lanes,
point a polished lens
at the freshly painted houses
we once called home,
raise a glass
in bars where our fathers once
found brief respite.

Friend
we have built our lives and fantasies
as well as we are able,
scorched past hurts
into level lines of words
now must leave our memories
in the cloying clay of
our Crumlin childhood.

Pauline Fayne

To Me Fella, A Letter

For Pauline Fayne

While I still wore slides and ribbons in my hair
I sat by the garden gate, reading comics
or dipped a wet brush into rectangles of colours
and trickles of blue, green and scarlet formed
under the lid of a tin paint box
bought in Corrigans shop.
You rode by on your Raleigh Chopper bike or
kicked a football up and down the road
two small people without thoughts of years to come
we went on living near the village.

At fourteen, I saw you, My Lord, again,
at the Core Disco. I, being bashful, never returned
your looks, asked to dance, I shook my head,
stared at the lights reflected on the wall
listened to Rod Stewart's Maggie May.

At fifteen I stopped scowling and heard Led Zeppelin
for the first time and desired the dust from our mantelpiece
to be mingled with the dust from your mother's sideboard,
Forever, and forever and forever.
Why should I climb the lookout on the lamp post
With a rope for swinging on?

At sixteen you departed, went into far Drum-Con-Dra,
by way of the dark lanes and across the river
of the swirling eddies and you have been gone five months.
The magpies make sorrowful noises overhead.

You dragged your feet when you went out,
The Evening Herald under your oxter,
on the path now, to the hall door, swards and mosses
and weeds have grown, the roots too deep to clear away.
The leaves fall early this Autumn, in wind.

Pairs of butterflies resting on the buddleia
in the back garden are already ochre in August.
They hurt me , I grow older.
If you are coming down the narrows
of the river Poddle,
please let me know beforehand
and I will come to meet you as far, as far,
as The-Stone-Boat-Lounge-and-Bar

Teri Murray

Note: *Based on 'The River Merchants Wife, A Letter'
by Chinese poet, Li Po, C750. Translation by Ezra Pound.*

Looceville House

Mr O'Neill's

'The Hucksters Shop'
my Granny would mutter.
a word I thought she invented,
as bizarre as
the stacked sofas
fake flowers,
prams and pictures that
defied gravity
in Mr O'Neill's stores.

He must have thought me
some kind of simpleton
as I joined the Friday queue
'never-never' card and coins in hand,
choking on suppressed giggles
at the sight of Mary in all her incarnations.

A glow in the dark Lady of Lourdes
hands outstretched to the china tea sets,
Our Lady of Consolation
enshrined on a Superser,
her Immaculate Medal
dangling from the handlebars
of a coveted bike,
a sorrowful, mock marble, plastic Pieta
that would subdue the smirk
of the most irreverent teen.

Pauline Fayne

8

The Holy Picture Man

Sold icons from a canvas bag
that rattled with plastic rosaries
and bottles of water
blessed at Knock
miraculous medals
on cheap blue threads
coiled like serpents in his hands

As he puzzled out the roads of Crumlin
Durrow, Kildare, Lismore,
named for cavities of monasteries,
Clonard, Clonfert, Clonmacnoise

When I still believed that
he was the Christ
hawking images of himself
from door to door.

Teri Murray

Crumlin Cross

The Somerville Soldier

At first she watched from the window,
the slanted cap, shiny boots and sure steps of the
soldier.
Soon ventured to the garden,
offered a shy salute,
thrilled at its return.

Began to trail him
on his walks
through avenue and field.
Shared a glimpse
of her treasured, ink blotted jotter
filled with drawings
of flags, flowers and birds.

Showed him where the corncrake hid,
pointed out the tiny red beak of the moorhen,
asked him for a 'real' tricoloured flag
and when he laughed agreement
begged a Union Jack as well

Knew, without understanding
in the sudden silence
that fell between them,
that soldiers and children were mismatched friends.

Pauline Fayne

Private Courtney

I wait for you still
at the curve of the world
where Windmill Lane
collides with Kildare Road

Straitjacketed in green wool
tunic slashed with flashes of
the Eastern Command
trousers creased as sharply
as my Grandmother's tongue

I escort you for the last few yards.
A solitary warrior
marching towards the war.

Teri Murray

The post box beside what was Candon's shop and post office

Under A Linnet's Wing

There was a lane at the side of
The Cinema, track pitted
and full of holes,
One day in late Autumn
I walked among the slippery stones.

The young man in front
turned around,
"How are ya?" he called,
"I'll be down that way"

I looked behind, sure
that there was someone else,
but he waited for me to catch up at the
open mouth of the gate.

I knew who he was,
grey duffle, the long boned, ascetic face
and American-style sneakers.
We all knew who he was,
young white atoms clustering
around a numinous black star

"What ya been up to?"
As if we had continued a conversation
from a minute before,
"Reading a bit" I mumbled.
How could I tell him of Christina Rosetti
Pablo Neruda , Langton Hughes,
Not to mention my own little tries at rhyme?

"Doin' a bit of jamming me'self,
trying to write the songs,
stringing together the few words."

So confident, tones so rich and full of life
I was content to be there and listen, for a
while.

At the far gate we parted,
"See ya" he said, with a smile and a
wave of his hand.
It had started to rain again,
he pulled up the woollen hood
of his coat and broke into a run,
scattering speckles of silver
along the length of Windmill Road.

Years later, I saw him on Grafton Street,
me, chasing unruly children
and weighed down with shopping,
but, he stopped for a moment and winked,
and I liked to think that he remembered,
the time he escorted a shy, tongue-tied girl
across the path in the park.

One day, maybe soon
we'll go home to Crumlin, if only
for just a rainy afternoon and he
will be singing...
The Boys Are Back In Town!

Teri Murray

Philo

For Michael O' Flanagan
(the cameraman)

Giggling teens
in 'budgie' jackets
trip hazard flares
and high wedge heels

We admired the daring
of the graffiti artist
who sprayed your name
along the village walls

Hoped to meet you

at the Star Cinema or Fusco's chipper,
swore The Black Eagles
would be world famous soon.

Today I watched again that film
of you running past our house
chasing your dreams down Somerville Avenue
and wished I had been in the garden

Shyly waving among the wallflowers
as you flashed your brilliant smile
at the cameraman,
striding towards stardom.

Pauline Fayne

Phil Lynott - The National Stadium 1972

The Breadman

Wearing his buff coloured working coat
and whistling at half past two in the afternoon,
Tommy always threw open the back doors
of the van and the smell of freshly baked dough
wafted down the road.

From pans, turnovers and batch loaves
stacked on wooden pallets
in our minds' eye
they were already neatly sliced
then plated on the kitchen table
and slathered with slabs of
golden butter.

Teri Murray

The Breadman Cometh

Eyes, skin and long buttoned coat
brown as the crusty loaves you carried -
I never learnt your name
but relished the scent
drifting down
our narrow avenue
that announced your arrival.

Too impatient to wait
until you reached our house
I would run towards you
hoping for hot turnovers
still steaming
on the wooden boards
of your van

Walk slowly back
gripping them triumphantly
like a prize
leaving not so discreet holes
in their doughy centre
that mother would pretend not to
notice.

Pauline Fayne

Glebe House

The Globe on Captains Road

for Brian McGovern

At the amphitheatre
in Waldron's back garden,
we balanced on an old plank
sipped juice from melted ice pops
munched Marietta biscuits.
We could have been in the Abbey Theatre
watching a performance of
O'Casey or Brecht.

The puppets on Paul Hanna's hands
projected sagas onto a sheet
flapping on the line:
Captain Boyle stumbling home
from Mooney's in the village;
Mother Courage catching
the early bus to do
a bit of a cleaning job;

Screamed at Missus Punch

      - tears blotting her papier-mâché face -
to hide the baby under the bed
away from her husband's
unrelenting fists;
booed at the Garda
as he tried to stop two women
tousling over a ball that flattened
antirrhinums and dented the symmetry of a privet hedge.

Warrior, magician, maid and hag
all the archetypes were there;
impersonating the neighbours,
exposing the quirks in our society
at the amphitheatre
in Waldron's back garden.

Teri Murray

Theatre of the Absurd

Each summer the audience returns,
carrying sun hats, dusty cushions and
warm pennies in sticky hands

Patiently accepting
well watered squash,
marietta biscuits
and cornflake sandwiches

As they wait
for conjurers, comedians
jugglers and dancers
to emerge from the dusty shed
in tablecloth cloaks
and ill-fitting costumes.

The drama varies little -
a juggler will drop the borrowed eggs
a dancer run home crying -
mistaking cheers and clapping
for sarcasm

And the final act stay
in the shed
singing from behind the door.

Pauline Fayne

"Christy Dunnes" Fruit and Vegetable shop

A Memory of my Father

In my memory it is always July
and I am back in 351 Captains Road
sneaking down the creaking stairs
knowing that below in the kitchen he is
brewing the tea.

In the sitting room, I fiddled
with the dials on the old Bush radio
red needle whizzed past exotic names
of places printed on the glass,
until the crackling noise stopped
and it was again tuned
into the frequency of RTE.

A violin played 'The Lark In The Clear Air',
and music like sunlight flooded
through Crumlin, Walkinstown, Drimnagh
and other Townlands.

We waited for Eamon Keane
to recite Kavanagh's poem
'Spraying the Potatoes',

A child of the city, I never learned
how to plant a seed in soil, tell
a swallow from a swift,
or predict the weather from the sky.

Yet, I was there with a knapsack sprayer
on that headland in Monaghan,
and knew even then
how blossomed stalks could weave a spell.

It is half-past-eight on a Sunday morning,
my father is alive, we are listening
to Ciarán Mac Mathúna's
'Mo Cheol Thu', and sipping our tea,
his laced with whiskey, mine
sugar-free.

Teri Murray

Visits

Twelve
the night I saw
the locked door handle turn,
heard footsteps
leather loud on the hard floor
of our empty hallway

Swallowed tears, fear and anger
at overheard mutterings
about 'the highly strung child'

Forty years on
I see a man at the village crossroads
street light glinting
on his prescription glasses,
walk towards my father

Before realising
he is gone - again.

Pauline Fayne

The Old Parochial School of St. Mary

Notes

I miss the notes around the rooms
in incongruous places,
written on the backs
of the torn packs of Player's No 6 boxes.

In her almost illegible script, it
was like a code between us,
most of my life,
I could never figure it out.

The shopping lists
the prices carefully totted up
by me, on days
when she could not go out,
hiding from callers,
under the table,
and I went to the village in her stead.

To see one of the Dunne sisters
weighing the half-stone of potatoes
in the metal lap of the scales,
the spices shaken from a dredger
on to the pork chops
in the window sizzling
like Brian Clarke the butchers red hair,
and Missus Brady, the chocolate bars
shimmering in silver wrappers.

And every week she kept ready for collection
in a bundle, under the counter
the Judy, the Mandy
and Spotlight Music Magazine.

But the one I remember most,
April 1977, just discharged
from The Coombe Hospital

I walked into the empty house,
propped on the mantelpiece
beside the wood enclosed clock
that chimed at the oddest of hours,

"Your sister gone off to get married,
Don't tell your Father!"

Teri Murray

Inscribed lintel above the doorway of Old St Mary's Church

Bogeyman

She learnt young
that he would visit
those not blanketed in sleep
before dark.

Risked it once
tight safe in father's arms
watching for the wishing star
until their whispered vigil
was stilled by mother's screams
eyes glazed with fear
of the silent man in black
echoing her footsteps
past the old church yard.

The plough would cut the night sky many times
before she saw it again,
while mother's fears
remained
constant as the moon.

Pauline Fayne

Villages like Crumlin

The moon was a slice
of silver
spangled stars danced on branches
where mythical apples
drops of gold in green skins
shimmered with old old light.

The knowledge of dreams
hoarded in seeds
tended by nymphs
and women like me
the watchful daughters
of the night

Who wander from lives untold
find shelter in the ripening orchard
of the soul and still never can conceive of the
alchemy that fuses fruits to trees.

Or why Gaia hoists her Autumn frock
and heaves a corset of branches
under a bodice of leaves
and squats on the thighs of the trees
trembling and immodest
and births the old old tainted
flesh from the belly of the Goddess.

Teri Murray

In Mooney's Field

She envied them
the tousle headed kids
with their brightly patched
'especially for play' clothes.

Eyed them
from behind the tied gates that
were her boundary.
While they climbed the orchard walls,
believed green apple sickness
was part of the fun,
as normal as peeing in the grass

The first time the gates were open
she ran with them,
shrieking her delight
as they bounced the fat baby
across the fields in his pram
until the wheel stuck in the ditch
and she clasped his heavy wetness tight

while they kicked and swore,
pulled it free to reveal
a rats nest,
angry small bodies
jumping towards them
before they ran screaming,
pram abandoned to its furry interlopers.

Home,
she tied the gates herself,
sometimes Mother was right.

Pauline Fayne

Mooney's Field

A Song For Pauline

for Kay, Marian, Ger
and Antoinette

Break the string-fold music's wing
Suppose Pauline had bade me sing
One way of love.

- Robert Browning

Even the Beatles
thought that you were so beautiful
singing their love words to you
from the meshed mouth
of a transistor radio
on your dinner hour
from Livingston and Spencers,
the clothing factory,
the hem of your hair
threading the embroidered leaves
of a privet hedge
summer sandals dangling
as you sat on the garden wall

David Bailey would have winked
as you flirted with the eye of his camera
        - like you did for yer man on the bike
            from Windmill Park -
as your fingers caressed
the bodice of a floral patterned dress that
you had fashioned for yourself.

When it came to style, Pauline Waldron,
you could have given the wans
In Paris, London or Milan
a run for their money

My clumsy fingers could never hold
a needle - all I could ever do was
stitch images into words.

But in the seam of the snagged
and tattered fabric that covers my heart
I will always be eleven
and you turning the wheel
of the sewing machine towards sixteen
even the Beatles thought
that you were so beautiful
and they were not the only ones, Hon.

Teri Murray

Crumlin Rose

You came loudly into my life,
high heels clattering in the night
seeking relief from the seeping coldness of
streets and strangers.

Later you would come quietly
to share my midnight meal,
watch the dawns approach
and whisper to me

Of the indignities of old men
who liked your skin to smell
of vanilla and chocolate,
of their marble cold hands,
of the heroin blazing through your veins,
of your ambitions

To stride confidently down catwalks
to place your name
like a hot fleeting kiss on
the lips of all those
who made you feel invisible.

You would achieve one goal -
your photo on the front page
your name headline news,
laid out in your coffin at sixteen in
your favourite pastel blue suit.

Pauline Fayne